Coming to CANADA

THE FRENCH

Sara Mitchell

Weigl

Published by Weigl Educational Publishers Limited
6325 10th Street SE
Calgary, AB T2H 2Z9

Website: www.weigl.ca

Library and Archives Canada Cataloguing in Publication

Mitchell, Sara, 1972-, author
    The French / Sara Mitchell.

(Coming to Canada)
Includes index.
Issued in print and electronic formats.
ISBN 978-1-4872-0152-4 (bound).--ISBN 978-1-4872-0153-1 (pbk.).--
ISBN 978-1-4872-0154-8 (epub)

    1. Canadians, French-speaking--History--Juvenile literature.
2. French--Canada--History--Juvenile literature. I. Title.

FC132.M58 2014   j971'.004114   C2014-904831-9
                                            C2014-904832-7

Printed in the United States of America in North Mankato, Minnesota
1 2 3 4 5 6 7 8 9 0 18 17 16 15 14

072014
WEP110614

Project Coordinator: Katie Gillespie
Art Director: Terry Paulhus

Photo Credits
Weigl acknowledges Getty Images, Alamy, Corbis, Newscom, and Dreamstime as
its primary image suppliers for this title.

We acknowledge the financial support of the Government of Canada through
the Canada Book Fund for our publishing activities.

CONTENTS

INTRODUCING THE FRENCH

From the early 1500s, France set out to become an international **colonial power**. Colonies could bring access to gold and other natural resources. France became interested in the lands in the north of North America in the hope of gaining wealth and **prestige**. The French established settlements such as Port-Royal, the capital of **Acadia**, and Quebec, the capital city of New France. In the centuries that followed, France would send many settlers, soldiers, traders, and **missionaries** to New France. They would profit from Canada's land and natural resources. A new **francophone** society would be built on Canadian shores.

When Jacques Cartier landed on the Gaspé Peninsula in 1534, he put up a large wooden cross with the French words *"Vive Le Roi de France"* written on it. This translates to "Long Live the King of France."

France was interested in the rich fishing waters of the Grand Banks, off the southeast coast of Newfoundland. By 1550, more than 100 ships were making regular fishing voyages across the Atlantic Ocean.

THE VOYAGES OF CARTIER

Jacques Cartier, a French explorer, made three trips to Canada between 1534 and 1543. On the first trip, he claimed Newfoundland and the Gaspé Peninsula in present-day Quebec for Canada. On the second trip, he sailed up the St. Lawrence River and visited First Nations settlements at Stadacona, present-day Quebec City, and Hochelaga, present-day Montreal. In 1541, Cartier returned to Canada for the final time. He brought with him 1,500 settlers and established a short-lived colony called Charlesbourg Royal near Stadacona. The settlers struggled, and the colony was closed down in 1543.

THE FUR TRADE

While New France did not have the gold that France had hoped for, it did have a plentiful supply of fur. In the years following Cartier's voyages, the fur trade between Canada and France developed quickly. Beaver fur, in particular, was very fashionable in Europe. It was used to make a high-quality fabric called felt. The European beaver had been hunted almost to extinction, so Canadian furs were highly sought-after and very valuable. Independent woodsmen called *coureurs de bois* travelled deep into the forests and explored the waterways. European goods such as metal pots and blankets were exchanged for beaver **pelts**.

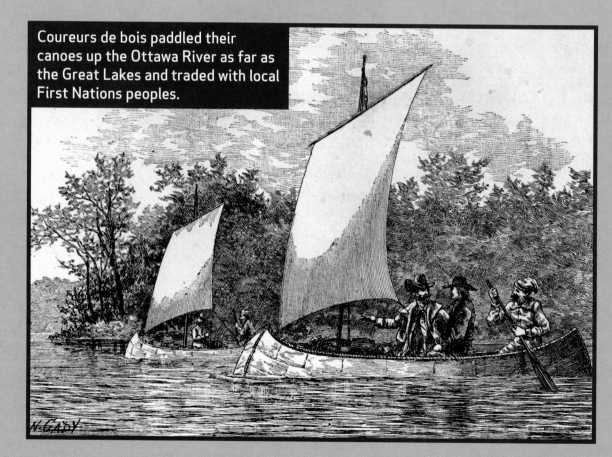

Coureurs de bois paddled their canoes up the Ottawa River as far as the Great Lakes and traded with local First Nations peoples.

FIRST NATIONS PARTNERS

The early French traders relied on the goodwill and support of First Nations peoples. The Aboriginal peoples were skilled hunters and knew how to survive in the harsh climate. They provided the traders with food, warm clothes, and traditional medicine. They also taught them how to build canoes and snowshoes, and how to find their way in the wilderness. France's main trading partners were the Algonquin and Huron Nations.

Around **200,000 pelts** were shipped from New France to Europe each year.

In 1600, Tadoussac, Quebec became the first European fur-trading post in Canada. Today, the original house and fur-trading post has been rebuilt as a museum.

NEW FRANCE

The French government was eager to establish New France as a permanent colony. In 1608, a French explorer named Samuel de Champlain led a group of colonists up the St. Lawrence River, where they constructed a **fortified** building on the site of present-day Quebec City. This was to become the first permanent settlement in New France, outside of Acadia. The early years of the Quebec colony were hard, and the population grew slowly. In 1633, Champlain became governor of New France. To protect the settlement from raids, Champlain entered into **alliances** with local First Nations. He supported the Huron in battles against the Iroquois. As a result, the Iroquois became enemies of the French.

Catholic priests began arriving in 1615 with two aims. The first was to convert First Nations peoples to Christianity. The second was to recreate European society in Canada.

Although New France was slow to grow, by 1759, it was a colony of over 60,000 people. Quebec was the main city, and the centre for both religious and government authority.

In 1627, the **Company of One Hundred Associates** was given the exclusive right to the fur trade of New France. In exchange, they had to bring over an average of 160 French settlers per year. Only Roman Catholics were allowed to **emigrate** to the colony. Catholic nuns soon established schools and hospitals in the main centres.

Sainte-Marie among the Hurons was a mission post built in 1638. It contained living quarters, a chapel, a hospital, and stables for animals.

THE ROYAL TAKEOVER

By 1660, New France was not growing fast enough. The population was still less than 3,000, and less than one percent of the land was being farmed. In 1663, the Company of One Hundred Associates gave up control of the colony to King Louis XIV. New France officially became a **province** of the French **Crown**. New France grew under direct royal control. Louis XIV extended the territory, supported settlement, and encouraged new businesses. Most importantly, he guaranteed the peace. Soldiers arrived to build forts where settlers would be safe from the attacks of the Iroquois. The king also created the position of intendant, to run the colony.

The first intendant of New France was Jean Talon. He dealt with the daily business of the colony, from collecting taxes to organizing the construction of roads and canals.

In 1663, Quebec City had a population of more than 500 people, living in about 100 homes. The city quickly outgrew its planned area and was overcrowded by 1700.

Young men often came to Canada as *engagés*, or indentured servants. This meant that their employer paid for their passage from France to the colony. In return, the engagés were required to work for a certain length of time for little or no money. This system often worked well, and the servants received training in skilled trades such as carpentry.

THE KING'S DAUGHTERS

To increase the number of women in the colony, the king of France sent ships carrying young women called *les filles du roi*, or the king's daughters. The king paid the cost of their voyage and provided them with a **dowry** of £50 each. It was hoped that they would find husbands among the local soldiers and settlers. From 1663 to 1673, more than 800 young women went to New France as part of this program.

DAILY LIFE

The French colonists wanted to make New France as much like their homeland as possible. They used a method of land ownership known as the seigneurial system. This was based on the system that had developed in France during the **Middle Ages**. Under this system, the king was the owner of all land and gave large areas to noblemen called *seigneurs*. The seigneurs then divided their land among tenant farmers, called *habitants*. The habitants paid taxes to the seigneur, gave him a portion of their harvest, and were required to work for the seigneur for three days every year, usually building roads.

About 75 to 80 percent of the population of New France lived as habitants until the mid-1800s.

LAND OWNERSHIP

Each seigneur kept a large section of his land for himself and his family. The rest of the land was divided into strips so that more settlers had access to the river. Settlers had to work hard to clear their land of trees before crops could be planted.

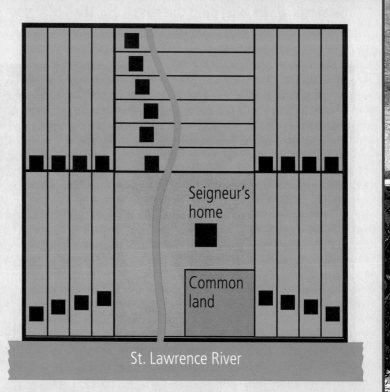

Seigneur's home

Common land

St. Lawrence River

Habitants grew wheat for bread and hay for their animals. They kept chickens, pigs, cows, sheep, and horses. Families were large, with as many as 15 children. Life in New France was hard work, but it was a better life than many of the colonists would have had in France. Wood for heating was plentiful, as were fish and wild animals for food.

Most children in New France did not go to school. They were kept busy helping their parents on their farms.

The people of New France were very sociable. They visited each other and had parties with good food, singing, and dancing.

THE FALL OF NEW FRANCE

As New France grew, so did the Thirteen British Colonies to the south. The settlers of these colonies became worried about the large French presence to the north. Many of them also wanted a piece of the rich farmland under French control. In 1754, American soldiers, led by Colonel George Washington, invaded French territory. This triggered the Seven Years' War, a fierce conflict between Great Britain and France for control of North America.

In 1759, the British troops, led by General James Wolfe, climbed the high cliff that protected Quebec City and defeated the French in the Battle of the Plains of Abraham.

In 1763, France finally declared defeat and signed the Treaty of Paris. New France became part of the British Empire. English-speaking settlers flooded into the region. This threatened the French-Canadian culture and way of life. In 1763, the British issued the Royal Proclamation. In this document, the land along the St. Lawrence River became the Province of Quebec, and the Maritime regions of New France were added to Nova Scotia. English law was introduced to make the area more attractive to British settlers. Under English law, only Protestants could take part in government, be a judge, or sit on a jury. This meant that the mainly Catholic French Canadians were excluded from having a say in how the province was run.

During the 1759 siege on Quebec, British soldiers burned **535** houses. More than **1,400** farmhouses in the countryside were also destroyed.

After the siege on Quebec in 1759, much of the city was reduced to rubble. The French buildings had been no match for the cannonballs of the British.

THE DEVELOPMENT OF LOWER CANADA

The first two British governors of the province of Quebec had respect for French Canadian traditions and beliefs. In 1774, the Quebec Act cancelled out most of the Royal Proclamation. It officially recognized the Catholic Church, and removed the ban on Catholics in government. However, less than a year after the Quebec Act was passed, war broke out in the Thirteen British Colonies to the south. The Americans demanded independence from Great Britain, which they won in 1783. Those Americans who had remained loyal to the British king, known as Loyalists, flooded into Quebec. French Canadians had to deal with large numbers of English-speaking settlers arriving in their homeland.

The Loyalists believed that Canada should have British laws and institutions. This meant that they were not always tolerant of the French Canadians.

The Loyalists made many demands of the British government. To solve the problem, Great Britain divided Quebec in half. The Constitutional Act of 1791 created the provinces of Upper Canada and Lower Canada. Upper Canada, present-day Ontario, would be English. Lower Canada, present-day Quebec, would be French. French Canadians were pleased with the new solution. They now had their own colony and could continue practising their own religion and culture.

1837–1838 REBELLIONS

Resentment between the French and the British led to a series of armed conflicts in Lower Canada from 1837 to 1838. After several battles, the British defeated the primarily francophone *Patriotes*. However, the French Canadians had been successful in achieving more representation in the government of their colony.

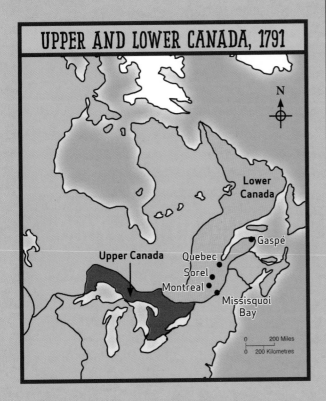

UPPER AND LOWER CANADA, 1791

Lower Canada

N

Gaspé

Upper Canada

Quebec
Sorel
Montreal

Missisquoi Bay

0   200 Miles
0   200 Kilometres

FRANCOPHONE CULTURE

One of the most important ways in which French-Canadian culture is defined is through language. French settlers brought the French language with them to Canada. However, after France lost its North American territories to Great Britain in 1763, francophones in Canada had limited contact with France. This division from their homeland, coupled with exposure to English and Aboriginal languages, had an influence on both French-Canadian language and culture. The physical landscape and climate of Canada have also had an impact. New words such as *toboggan* were introduced. Building styles were modified to suit the Canadian winter. New meats, fruits, and vegetables were added to the French-Canadian diet.

Both French and English became **official languages** of Canada in 1969 through the Official Languages Act. This act was introduced to support the use of French. The vast majority of francophones live in Quebec, where French has been the only official language since 1977. However, there are francophones living in every province and territory of Canada.

PIERRE ELLIOTT TRUDEAU 1919–2000

Pierre Elliott Trudeau was a Liberal prime minister of Canada from 1968–1979 and 1980–1984. From Montreal, Trudeau was a strong supporter of **bilingualism**. He brought in the Official Languages Act in 1969. This cemented Canada as an officially bilingual nation. In 2014, Pierre Trudeau topped a list of the 10 most inspiring Canadians over the last 150 years.

Cinderella

May 3

Rated G, 1h 45min

2:30pm & 6:30pm

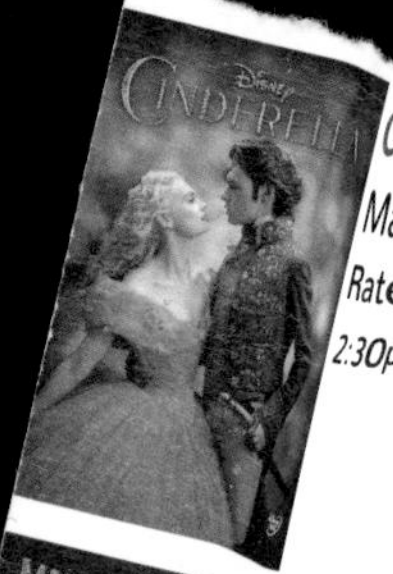

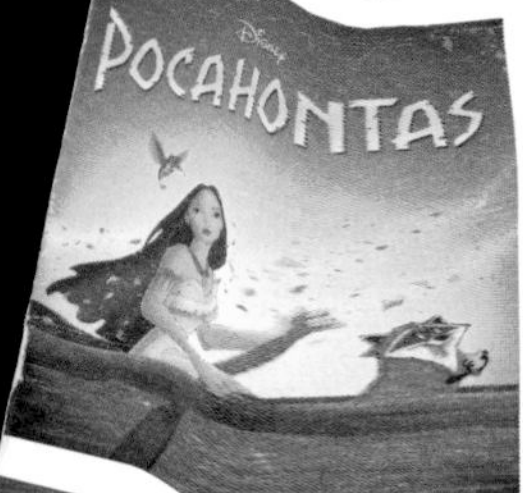

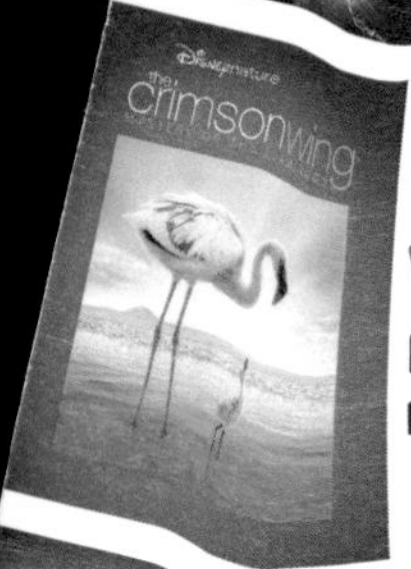

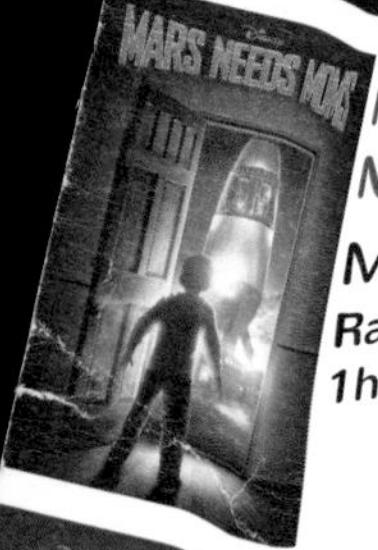

Mars Needs Moms

May 10

Rated PG

1h 28min

DisneyNature: The Crimson Wing

May 17

Rated G, 1h 18min

Pocahontas

May 24

Rated G, 1h 21min

barrielibrary...

48 Dean Avenue, Barrie

Friday Flicks
6:30pm

Bring some **popcorn** and join us for **popular** and entertaining movies, perfect for the whole family. This month we are excited to feature
The Secret Life of Pets!

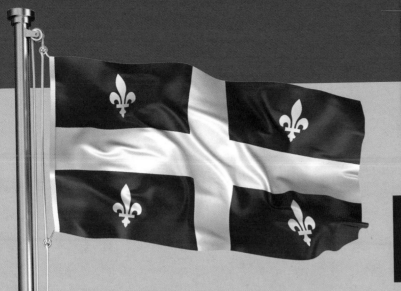

Since 1948, the flag of Quebec has been the *Fleurdelisé*, which symbolizes Quebec's French origins.

SAINT-JEAN-BAPTISTE DAY

Quebec's National Holiday, Saint-Jean-Baptiste Day, is celebrated every year on June 24th. This important French-Canadian holiday has been celebrated with street parades and bonfires since 1843. It has been an official holiday in Quebec since 1977. Originally from France, Saint-Jean-Baptiste Day is also celebrated as a festival of French-Canadian culture in other Canadian provinces and the United States.

FRENCH-CANADIANS TODAY

French-Canadian culture has developed over 400 years of settlement. Today, French Canadians are an independent people who are proud of their distinctive **heritage**. Francophone culture is supported by the Canadian Broadcasting Corporation (CBC), which broadcasts French-language news programs, dramas, films, and sporting events. French-language newspapers are read by many francophones across the country.

Montreal is the home of the international circus, *Cirque du Soleil*. Imaginative, energetic, and unusual, Cirque du Soleil is an example of French-Canadian culture that is enjoyed around the world.

French-Canadians are also known for appreciating great food. Classic French-Canadian dishes include meat pies, butter tarts, pea soup, and *poutine*, which is French fries and flavoured gravy mixed with cheese curd.

Quebec is well known for its festivals. These include the Gatineau Hot Air Balloon Festival and the highly popular Quebec Winter Carnival. The two-week-long carnival is the largest winter carnival in the world. It includes skiing, zip-lining, ice sculptures, sleigh rides, skating, and a spectacular ice castle. While 85 percent of French-Canadians live in Quebec, there are many other centres across Canada with well-established French populations. Across the nation, French-Canadians have contributed largely to making Canada the vibrant, **multicultural** country it is today.

Montreal is Canada's **second largest city** and one of the largest francophone cities outside of France.

From the beginning of New France, settlers got together to overcome winter's hardships with fun and festivities. Since the first large Winter Carnival in Quebec City in 1894, the annual festival has grown to be a highlight for both locals and tourists.

FRENCH QUIZ

1 Which French explorer made three trips to Canada between 1534 and 1543?

2 How many pelts were shipped from New France to Europe each year?

3 Who became the governor of New France in 1633?

4 In 1627, which commercial enterprise was given the exclusive right to the fur trade of New France in exchange for bringing in settlers?

5 How many filles du roi, or king's daughters, were brought to New France between 1663 to 1673?

6 What were the tenant farmers of New France called?

7 In which year did New France become part of the British Empire?

8 In which year was Canada divided into Upper Canada and Lower Canada?

9 Which Canadian prime minister was responsible for making French one of Canada's two official languages?

10 Which Canadian province is home to the largest winter carnival in the world?

Answers
1. Jacques Cartier
2. around 200,000
3. Samuel de Champlain
4. the Company of One Hundred Associates
5. more than 800
6. habitants
7. 1763
8. 1791
9. Pierre Elliott Trudeau
10. Quebec

KEY WORDS

Acadia: a former French colony established in 1604 in the area that is now the Maritime provinces, part of Quebec, and Maine, United States

alliances: partnerships formed for mutual benefit, especially between countries

bilingualism: the ability to speak two languages fluently

colonial power: a country with many colonies, or territories in distant lands

Company of One Hundred Associates: a French trading and colonization company that operated from 1627 to 1663

Crown: the monarch or head of state

dowry: property or money brought by a bride to her husband

emigrate: to leave one's own country to settle permanently in another

fortified: equipped with defensive features for protection against attack

francophone: French-speaking

heritage: the traditions, achievements, and beliefs that are part of the history of a group or nation

Middle Ages: the period of European history from about 400 to 1500

missionaries: people sent by a church to do religious work in a territory or foreign country

multicultural: people from many different backgrounds living together in society

official languages: languages that are given a special legal status in a country or province and are used within the government, schools, and courts of law in that area

Patriotes: members of the *Parti Patriote* political group in Lower Canada from the early 1830s to 1840

pelts: animal skins with the fur or hair still on them

prestige: honour or status among others

province: a territory outside a country, but under the control of that country

INDEX

FURTHER RESEARCH

Many books and websites provide information about the French. To learn more about this topic, borrow books from the library, or search the internet. Check out some of the following websites to discover more interesting facts about the French.

Take a virtual tour of the Fortress of Louisbourg and learn more about the experiences of French settlers in the eighteenth century at: www.fortressoflouisbourg.ca

Discover more about the key events that helped shape the history of Quebec City at: www.ville.quebec.qc.ca/EN/touristes/connaitre/histoire/index.aspx

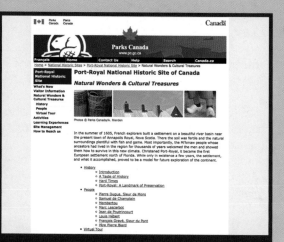

Find out more about the early French settlement, Port-Royal, at: www.pc.gc.ca/eng/lhn-nhs/ns/portroyal/natcul.aspx